MW01484320

Coaching Questions

Ask Powerful Questions
Develop Coaching Mindset
Improve The Way You Lead

By Jack Davies

"Coaching is unlocking a person's potential to maximize their own performance. It's helping them to learn rather than teaching them."

Tim Gallwey

Copyright 2017© Jack Davies

All rights reserved. No part of this guide may be reproduced in any form without permission in writing from the publisher except in the case of brief quotations embodied in critical articles or reviews.

ISBN-13: 978-1548742478

ISBN-10: 1548742473

Legal & Disclaimer: The information contained in this book and its contents is not designed to replace or take the place of any form of medical or professional advice; and is not meant to replace the need for independent medical, financial, legal or other professional advice or services, as may be required. The content and information in this book have been provided for educational and entertainment purposes only.

The content and information contained in this book have been compiled from sources deemed reliable, and it is accurate to the best of the Author's knowledge, information, and belief. However, the Author cannot guarantee its accuracy and validity and cannot be held liable for any errors and/or omissions. Further, changes are periodically made to this book as and when needed. Where appropriate and/or necessary, you must consult a professional (including but not limited to your doctor, attorney, financial advisor or such other professional advisor) before using any of the suggested remedies, techniques, or information in this book.

Upon using the contents and information contained in this book, you agree to hold harmless the Author from and against any damages, costs, and expenses, including any legal fees potentially resulting from the application of any of the information provided by this book. This disclaimer applies to any loss, damages or injury caused by the use and application, whether directly or indirectly, of any advice or information presented, whether for breach of contract, tort, negligence, personal injury, criminal intent, or under any other cause of action.

You agree to accept all risks of using the information presented inside this book.

You agree that by continuing to read this book, where appropriate and/or necessary, you shall consult a professional (including but not limited to your doctor, attorney, or financial advisor or such other advisor as needed) before using any of the suggested remedies, techniques, or information in this book.

Table Of Contents

Introduction

When it comes to getting the best out of life - whether in your life or from your team, there is no doubt that good coaching can play a pivotal role. Getting it right is about learning how to motivate yourself and others in a way that works. It means listening to yourself and others rather than just speaking to them. The good coach knows that they may not have all the answers.

You learn the basic elements of coaching to help you take your achievement, and, where you can apply, that of others around you or your team, to the next level. We will work on knowing what questions to ask, how to set accountability goals and how to ensure that the process is effective. You will also learn not only how to ask the appropriate questions but also how to listen to the answers given.

Most importantly, a life coach cannot professionally guide you through a sticky situation or a rough time if they have never experienced struggles themselves. A life coach can be considered good, if he or she has a positive outlook on life, and practically applies it.

If you want to be a life coach, but you freak out when you think that someone has grabbed your parking spot, but advise her clients that divorce can be a helpful step to grow personally, you are not genuine. Faking positive outlook will not help your client.

Another important factor that life coach should take care is how he is organizing his life. If you say to your client that you will call, but you fail to do so, then it is a red flag that he is not totally in control of his life, and should probably not be entrusted with your life.

All life coaches should be properly licensed. Your advice to your client could make or break his life. Hence, it is crucial for a life coach to be knowledgeable and well-trained in this promising career.

Good coaching is a simple and cost-effective way to zero in on what is important in your personal life and your business life. With the right encouragement, yourself and your team can go from muddling by to excelling and, after reading this book, and you will know exactly how to provide the necessary support and encouragement.

Life coaching is something related to the questions like what does it mean, what you want to do in your life etc. It is a democracy of solving the problems of the people. Solving your problem is not difficult as you might think sometimes. Coaching is most important whether it is for business, career, and relationship, etc. Coaches are specialized to enhance the lifestyle and to remove the emotional stress. In this book, I would discuss some of the guidelines to make your life better.

To be considered an effective life coach, one has to know what to do, know how to help, and of course, know which questions to ask.

CHAPTER 1 - Why Talk Less?

When it gets to coaching it is important to establish yourself as a trustworthy coach. This may seem a little strange – after all, surely after you've read this book you'll simply be able to call yourself a coach? It is a bit more complicated than that.

As a coach, if you hope to get the best out of yourself and others, you'll need to create a more nurturing environment – you'll need to create an environment that fosters trust and respect if you hope for your efforts to bear fruit and lead to success.

When Coaching Yourself

Believe it or not, it is usually hardest to create this nurturing environment when it comes to self-development. Think about it for a second – who is the person that you are hardest on? How many times do you criticize yourself for mistakes that you have made? Are you as hard on your team or those around you as you are on yourself? I seriously doubt it.

We have a tendency to be especially critical when it comes to ourselves – even when we make mistakes that we would readily forgive in others. You need to break out of that cycle if you want to up your game.

You need to be a non-judgmental mentor for yourself, and this means actively stopping the constant self-critique. Every time you catch yourself wanting to self-chastise, you need to stop and give yourself a break.

While we do need to do some self-analysis to be able to grow, constant negative reinforcement will only erode our self-confidence and leave us fearful of taking risks needed to grow.

When Coaching a Team

When it comes to coaching a team, you need to understand that there is a difference between talking on your team and working with them to help them improve. I used to work for a large company, and I remember being required to attend many "coaching" sessions. Some were quite motivating, but what I remember most is that in all events, we had people telling us what to do.

Needless to say, the positive effects of these training sessions were short-lived. In addition to this, we were subjected to intensive "coaching" in order to improve sales. What this amounted to was having to submit sales figures twice a day and attending a meeting once a week, which in reality boiled down to being "name and shame" sessions. Our regional manager's style of motivation involved telling us that if we didn't like it, we knew where the door was!

Needless to say, all that these sessions accomplished was to make the attendees miserable. No one felt that they could raise issues they were facing for fear of being told that they were trying to make excuses, and consequently staff turnover was high.

In the long run, this kind of negative coaching costs organizations a lot regarding a reduction in productivity and a greater cost in hiring and training – and then all of the money spent on training an individual went to waste when they inevitably left!

If, on the other hand, the regional manager had of worked on building trust with the staff and creating a positive environment, the rewards regarding innovation and productivity would have been tangible. Instead of being the name and shame sessions they were, these could have been productive, problem-solving sessions.

Whether you are coaching a team or coaching yourself, it is important that you respect the individual or individuals and foster an environment that facilitates growth and development rather than one that is based on negative, competitive elements.

You need to set measurable and clearly defined goals. A lot of people just charge into coaching without having a clearly defined goal and end up being dissatisfied with the results.

By setting what you want to achieve, and defining it clearly, you are giving yourself a much better chance of succeeding – you can then tailor your plan to your specific objectives and will be able to monitor your success against clear milestones as you progress.

For example, let us say that you want to improve sales in your organization. That is a pretty broad goal, and frankly, one that is easily met – all you need is one extra sale, and your goal is met. Because it is such a nebulous goal, you are bound to meet with mediocre results.

On the other hand, if you set a clear target of increasing the sales of a particular product by 10%, you are much more likely to be able to succeed because you have set a clearly definable goal.

CHAPTER 2 - Effective Questions For A Coaching Model

Coaching is going to require that you ask many questions, the skill is to do so in a way that it does not come across as an interrogation. Generally speaking, there are three types of questions that you will find useful, and we will cover each of these in detail in this chapter:

- Curious Questions
- Clarifying Questions
- Possibility Questions

With an arsenal of these questions at your disposal, you will find that getting the information and responses that you require from those you are mentoring will be a lot easier. The main key to getting these questions right is to phrase them in a non-judgmental way, a way that is going to build the relationship and trust rather than destroy it. For example, "Why did you let the whole team down?" is a question that is bound to elicit a defensive response because it seems accusatory. A better approach would be, "What went wrong on the project?"

Curious Questions

When it comes to curious questions, you need to be particularly careful in their phrasing, or they may come off as accusatory. Curious questions start off with the following:

1. How?
2. What?
3. Why?
4. When?
5. Supposing?

Curious questions should always be:

- Short and sweet – keep it to a maximum of 10 words.

- Concisely stated – Within the word count allowed, do ensure that you make it clear what you want to be answered.

- No "Yes" or "No" answers – leave the question open-ended to allow your mentee to expand upon their answer and explain their reasons more fully. This will help you to empathize with them better. You may also find that looking at things from a whole new angle sheds interesting light on the situation.

Now that you know the essentials of what your curious questions should be, it is time to talk a little on the phrasing of the questions.

As mentioned above, the last thing that you want to do is to put the person on the defensive so do take some time to compose the questions before you set them. If your mentee is on the defensive, they will keep looking for ways to justify their actions/ answers, and this will not help anyone come to a better solution.

For example, "Why are you always so late getting to work?" is going to put your employee on the defensive immediately. On the other hand, you could say, "What reasons would you attribute to a delay in getting to work?" In both cases, you are asking the same thing but the second question is a softer approach.

Think about the question before you ask it and view it from your employees point of view – how would you react if you were them? Be creative when phrasing your questions.

During the conversation that ensues, empathetic listening comes into play. Pick up on a phrase or two in the answers and build upon that in the next question. That way, you get more of the information that you want without coming across as an inquisitor.

Do set this session at a time when you have enough time to devote to it. You must ask no more than one question at a time and be able to consider the responses given and your responses as well.

Also, be careful that you do not go into too much detail explaining your question or give hints as to what answers you were hoping to get – you want honest answers, not what the mentee is hoping you want to hear.

Also be careful about how you react to the answers given – even when you don't agree with them. If you get defensive when issues are brought up, your mentee will no longer feel comfortable raising issues with you. If on the other hand, you demonstrate some empathy, your mentee will be encouraged to raise more issues, allowing you to get to the heart of the problem.

Clarifying Questions

It would be great if we could just ask the right curious questions and get all our answers that way. Unfortunately, in the real world, it just does not work that way. There are going to be times when you will need more details – where perhaps the mentee has not explained themselves properly or you do not fully understand the answer or where you need them to provide more details. For these times, clarifying questions are vital.

The aim here is to clarify what you have been told. For example, "Am I to understand that the bus service in your area is very unreliable?" You could also take this chance to ask more probing questions. For example, "Is it possible to find an alternate means to get to work?"

Again, the aim here is to ask questions that are more open-ended. By this stage in the conversation, however, you should have built up some trust so you can afford to be a little more direct. (While still taking care not to put the person on the defensive.) Concentrate on the matter at hand rather than the person when formulating your clarifying questions.

Possibility Questions

If you want the mother-load of information, possibility questions are the best way to get it. The aim here is to get more information and perhaps to lead your mentee in the direction of coming up with a solution. For example, you could ask when training should start. By making them consider and give input on the possibilities, you automatically make it easier for them to buy into the solution as well because they helped to come up with it.

So yes, again here we want open-ended questions, but we do want to take a more targeted approach. Let's look at the question, "When

31

should training start?". While it is a valid question, it is not targeted enough – you could end up discussing the matter all day.

Now while your mentee could give any answer to the possibility questions posed to them, you can get a more targeted approach by steering the question properly. And by this, I mean giving some guidelines regarding the scope of the answer – not trying to make them give you the answer that you want.

The most useful aspect of possibility questions is that they can encourage your mentee to come up with the solution on their own, seemingly without your interference. This can make a great deal of difference when it comes to being able to implement the solution as mentees will think it was their idea.

There are a couple of ways to drive the conversation – you could pose the question and give a few possible solutions, or you could pose the question and give the options of different answers.

For example, "Would you like to sign up now or do you want some time to talk to your family about it?"

When it comes to possibility questions be guided by your mentee and what you know about them – if they are prone to over-analyze things, apply stricter targeting; if they are hard to draw into a conversation, apply a looser rein.

CHAPTER 3 - Be Supportive and Define The Topic And Needs

Ask ten people what a good coach is, and you are likely to get ten different answers. For the most part, though, we judge the coach on the results that they achieve. That said though; there are a range of traits that you have to develop if you want to be a top notch coach.

You Need to be Patient and Persevere

Sometimes you will be able to break through to someone at the first meeting, but this is the exception rather than the norm. You need to accept that the coaching process can be a slow one – you need to gain your mentee's trust before you can make real strides forward and this might be easier said than done at times.

It is also going to mean, at times, explaining things over and over again to people who just don't get it. If you cannot do this without losing your cool, you will need to work on yourself a bit before starting to coach others.

You also need to be willing to see things through – even when it seems as though your mentee is making very little progress. You never know when that final breakthrough might occur and you do not want to miss it.

If your mentee sees that you give up with only a little effort, they will believe that they do not deserve the work and that it is not worthwhile to try and persevere in life in general.

Admit that, no matter how good you are at coaching, there are going to be some mentees that learn fast and others that don't – learn to tailor your approach and patience accordingly.

You Need the Respect and Trust of Your Mentees

For coaching to be successful, your mentees need to respect you as a person and trust you as well. Note, I did not say that they had to like you – you do not have to be the drinking buddy that staggers home with them after a night out. You do, however, have to be there for them when you say you will be.

There is a saying, "Talk the talk and walk the walk." You need to lead by example and show your mentees that you live by the principles that you are teaching them. How much credibility will you have left if you walk onto the field with a cigarette in one hand a chili-cheese fries in the other?

The same goes for emotional coaching as well. For example, that you are teaching your mentees about the importance of being patient. Afterward, you go to the store and start fuming about how long the line is and how slow the cashiers are – if one of your mentees were to see you, how much credibility would you lose?

Fair or not, when you are coaching others to improve themselves, you have to hold yourself to a higher standard, and you do have to practice what you preach in a consistent manner.

If your mentees know that you are there for them when you say that you will be, that you follow through on promises and that you are fair, they will start to trust and respect you.

Your goal as a coach is to get them to respect and trust you enough that they want to follow your advice or even aspire to be like you.

You Need to be Supportive

This is one of those common-sense skills, but it is amazing how many coaches forget about it, especially as time goes by. Being supportive means taking the good with the bad and not being judgmental about it. You need to create a safe space so that your mentee knows that, even if they screw up, they can discuss it with you and they need to know that they can safely raise issues with you.

It's a bit like having a best friend who is dating someone that you dislike. You might mention something to your friend, but you end up tolerating the significant other for your friend's sake. Should they break up, you are there to support your friend and, if you are a good friend, to bite back on the, "I told you so."

In the end, a good coach points the mentee in the right direction, but the mentee needs to make the final decision about what to do. They need to know that you will support them either way.

At least in part – you cannot teach people something that you do not know. For example, it would be a little silly to take over coaching a baseball team when you know nothing about the game.

Now, that does not mean that you need to know everything about the job that your mentee is doing, but it does mean that you need to know the techniques that you will be teaching backward and forwards. You should show your mentee how to adapt these techniques to suit themselves and how to apply them in different situations.

You need a Contingency Plan

Jumping straight into coaching without doing any planning drastically reduces your chances of success. Work out a rough idea of what you will be covering and when and review periodically regarding the progress that your mentee is making. Once you get to know your mentee better, it becomes easier to make decisions on the fly, but until you get to that point, you better have a plan in place and a Plan B as well.

You Need to Be Able to Monitor Performance Against Specific Measurables

You as a coach do need to set up two sets of accounting systems – one for yourself and one for your mentee. Find ways to measure ongoing progress so that you can see whether or not your coaching style has been effective or not.

Also set up measurable goals for your mentees so that you can see whether or not they are progressing. These goals will also help to inspire them to perform better.

The Ability to Get People to Think for Themselves

In the past, coaching meant telling people what they needed to do and how they needed to think. Research has shown that this method has only limited success. In one study, one group was told exactly what to eat to lose weight – they had no opportunity to discuss this and were not told why. The second group was treated; differently, they were presented with information on how certain foods helped with weight loss and the long-term consequences of not losing the weight. They were presented with the basic guidelines for a healthy diet but the choice of foods etc. was left to them.

Guess which group did better. Contrary to what you might think, participants in both groups lost about the same amount of weight over a four-week period. The difference in the number of dropouts was significantly higher in the first group, however.

Interestingly enough, when a follow-up was done three months later, it was found that the second group had performed significantly better when it came to maintaining the weight loss and a healthier lifestyle.

If you can get people to look at the issues being tackled critically and get them to understand the consequences of action or inaction, you should be able to leave them to make the right decision on their own.

And that is coaching gold right there – if your mentee has figured out for themselves that your answer is correct and that it will benefit them, they are going to get behind the process and give their very best.

Some coaches get annoyed when they have mentees who constantly ask them why their way is better or why it works. I love those mentees because I know that I have gotten their attention. And, quite frankly, if you cannot explain why what you are proposing works and what the benefit for the mentee is, you are wasting your time.

For most of us, the, "What's in it for me" drive is the strongest motivating factor.

CHAPTER 4 - Establish Impact and Assigning Accountability

I briefly spoke about the importance of having a plan in place and having clear, measurable targets to achieve for both you and your mentee. In this chapter, we will go into these concepts in greater detail.

Plan to Win and to Fail

Yes, I know – we should be positive and plan for the win, but the truth is that having a plan in place to deal with failure is a lot more useful. We think and hope that everything will go alright, but what if it does not? With any luck, you won't even need the plan but, if you do, it will be there for you to use.

Take a lesson from the banks during the sub-prime market scandal and subsequent crash of 2008. It was inconceivable that a large corporate like Lehman Brothers would collapse and so most businesses did not prepare for such an eventuality. PIMCO, on the other hand, spent some time formulating a plan of action should Lehman Brothers collapse. When Lehman Brothers did collapse, PIMCO was one of the few companies that had planned for the eventuality and, as a result, they were able to save their clients a lot of money.

Planning to win is fairly simple, take your mentee's ultimate goal and their proposed timeline and break it down into small, manageable steps that will work for your mentee regarding their current circumstances and personality. The ultimate goal is to make it as easy as possible for your mentee to build the skills and traits needed to succeed.

The tasks that you set should start out simple and build regarding complexity and difficulty as your mentee progresses.

Planning to fail is a little less fun but just as important. Take a look at your overall plan and consider what might go wrong. What if your mentee fails their exam or doesn't win the key race? How will you recover your plan from there?

Set Timelines

I read somewhere once that a list of goals without a specific time frame to complete them in was no more than a wish list, and this is very true. Part of your job as a coach is to encourage your mentee to reach their goals and this entails putting a very real timeline on things.

It is important, however, to ensure that the timeline is realistic and to do regular reviews to ensure that it remains realistic.

Accountability and Responsibility

This means setting guidelines in place to ensure that everyone understands what their role is and what they are meant to be doing. The mentee has to understand that achieving the improvement that they require is going to take some work and the coach has to understand that they have a responsibility to monitor the progress of the mentee.

Once you have formulated your plan to win, see what responsibilities will need to be assigned to the mentee and yourself. Set yourself a timeline to review progress and to see how things are going.

Once you know what you will be taking your mentee with, you need to set accountability for the tasks – i.e. What will your mentee need to do and when will they need to do it by?

As regards your overall plan and how you convey it to your mentee, a lot will depend on your mentee themselves. Are you going to need to lead them so that they can find their answers? If so, it may not be the best bet to let them know the full plan outright. In this case, give them a broad overview of what you will be doing without going into too many specifics and assign them the first task.

Depending on your mentee, it may even be necessary to take this accountability a step further – perhaps they need to give you regular progress reports. Being accountable to someone else can be a huge motivating factor. Take the Weigh fewer meetings, for example. Once a week the various groups get together, and everyone gets up and weighs themselves in front of the whole group. This is an example of accountability – except that it is not just accountable to one person but a whole group. It works because you do not want to let others down or be embarrassed. It can also work for those who are highly competitive.

CHAPTER 5 - Reviewing Progress and Changing Course

Most people love the planning phase of things and think that, once that has been done, the hard work is over. Unfortunately, putting the plan into effect is only the first phase – you will need to do periodic reviews to ensure that the plan is effective and that things are going as planned.

When to Review

It seems to make sense that you set your reviews up just after the target date for goals so that you can see exactly how things went. This is a valid approach, but it could be a case of too little too late. What if things are not working out as you planned? If you leave it until the target deadline is reached and only review it then, you have wasted time and probably demotivated your mentee to boot.

It is better to do a review at about a quarter of the way through, another at a half, and a third, if necessary at three-quarters of the way through. What I like to do, also, is to check with my mentee a few days after the program has been instituted to see how they are coping with the change.

This may sound like a lot of work regarding reviews to be done, but it is especially important when starting off with your mentee and should be continued with until you know for sure that they are coping with your style of motivation and coaching. If you switch up styles or try something new, go back to this regular reviewing schedule.

Some reviews are good, so more are even better right? Up to a point. Remember me talking about my experience working for a large corporate. We had to submit sales figures twice daily so that management could review our progress and had to go for a weekly sales meeting as well. The weekly meeting on its own would have been annoying but okay. Having to submit figures twice daily was not only an intrusion and waste of time, but it had the opposite of the desired effect. The theory was that submitting the figures in this manner would motivate us more and lead to greater productivity – what it did, however, was sap morale and cause anxiety. Within three years, every single member of that sales team, I included, had left the company.

The system was scrapped soon after that because it was clear that it wasn't working. In the interim, however, they wasted three years simply because they didn't want to course correct.

What to Review

There is more to these reviews than just seeing how your mentee is progressing. You also need to touch base with them to see how things are going and how they are feeling about the progress that they are making.

Often we tend to look at success as the ultimate goal and ignore the journey that it takes to get there. You ensure that you are not putting undue pressure on your mentee as you move forward and that their goals have not changed over time.

It's kind of like what we see played out over and over again – you have a young boy whose parents want the best for them. They want him to be a sports star, let's say in baseball so they hire him a trainer or make him practice every day after school, whether he wants to or not. If being a star baseball player is his dream as well, this could work out well for him. If it is not, he is going to end up being miserable and probably hating baseball and his parents to boot.

I was ecstatic, for about a week. Then I started to realize that the position was not all that I had hoped for. I stuck it out for another four years, all the while becoming more and more miserable. You see, over time, I had changed – I had achieved what I wanted to, but because of this change, there was no satisfaction in it for me. Despite all the time spent studying and building my career, I decided that the time had come for me to resign and try something else. Again, everyone told me I was doing the wrong thing. Again, it turned out to be the best course of action for me.

If your mentee decides that they want to change direction, you need to try and support them in that decision.

Course Corrections in Need

There are times when you are going to come up with the most outstanding plan, one that simply cannot fail. One that you know will succeed. You do your reviews as you go along but are not seeing the results that you feel that you should. It must be something that the mentee is doing wrong, mustn't it?

It's a tough one to accept, but not every plan that we think is perfect is going to work out for our mentees. When it gets to the actual execution of the plan, things could go wrong, and we need to accept this and move along, changing the plan as necessary.

Dealing with Failures

As a coach, it can be downright disheartening when you put your all into it, and your mentee fails. It is tempting to blame them outright for the failure and let them know how badly they let you down. This is only going to damage the relationship that you have built, and so you have to be cautious about how you deal with failures.

It also bears remembering that your mentee is probably just as disappointed and also feeling guilty for letting you down. How you deal with failures is just as instrumental in your mentee's ultimate success.

The first thing to do is to be as non-judgmental as possible and to try and ascertain why the plan failed. Speak to your mentee, asking curious questions such as, "What were the difficulties that you encountered."

Once you have established what the problem was, you can tweak your plan so that you can prepare your mentee better in future.

Dealing with Successes

Of course, there will also be some successes along the way, and it is important that you and your mentee do celebrate these as well. When setting up your plan, do make a note of how the two of you will celebrate successes. When speaking about the tasks or goals with your mentee, it can serve as good motivation to inform them on what you are planning when they succeed.

It may seem odd, but successes may also call for a rethink of the overall plan. If you find that your mentee is progressing at a faster rate than expected, you might want to consider shortening the timeline – after discussing it with them, of course.

Whether you are course correcting due to success or failure, it is important to restart the reviewing process again – check in with your mentee to ensure that the new track is working for them and check back with them regularly.

Bonus

Taking an action

Taking some relevant action will help you to fight against worries, and you will be able to fix your problems. All you need to think about the best solution. I have a very good example. If your home is in the great need of repair and you are worried about the damages of your home from natural disaster strikes then instead of worrying about the disaster strikes, repair your home strong and powerful against the potential disaster. This is a best possible solution, or we can say relevant action.

Get the proper help you are in great need

There are some people who don't want to take the help of others. You must get some help if you need. If you think that you need some help, then consider the help of your friends and family members.

Breathe deeply to get the solution of any problem

You must hold breath slowly to control the heart rate and to calm your nerves. Take a long walk with your close friend. Few minutes of meditation and yoga is best to reduce the stress. At that moment you will feel yourself out of all worries.

Write it down what you think or what you want to do in your life

Having a personal diary is best to decrease your worries and stress on a daily basis. Open your diary, take a pen and write all worries of your mind on it. You should try to be very clear and specific like why exactly you are tensioned. Always motivate yourself for doing something very good in life.

Some of your tensions are helpful because they are related to your duties and responsibilities. Thanks for reading this post sincerely.

Conclusion

Whether you are coaching yourself or coaching someone else, you now have the basic tools that you need to get started.

Possibly the best part of the experience for me is that you never really stop learning and improving yourself in the process. I am often amazed at the insights of some of the people that I coach and am fascinated by the different perspectives that I learn about.

Coaching is not always easy, but there is nothing quite like knowing that you have helped someone else reaches for their star. At the end of the day, you have everything to gain and little to lose.

All that's left for me to say now is that there is no time like the present for you to get out there and get started. Expect to make mistakes along the way and view them as learning experiences, and you will soon find that you are a top class coach.

"Probably my best quality as a coach is that I ask a lot of challenging questions and let the person come up with the answer."

Phil Dixon

P.S. Thank you for reading this book. If you've enjoyed this book, please don't shy, drop me a line, leave a review or both on Amazon. I love reading reviews and your opinion is extremely important for me.

Made in United States
Orlando, FL
03 February 2025

58110569R00044